JELLYFISH TO INSECTS

Design	David West
	Children's Book Design
Editorial Planning	Clark Robinson Limited
Picture researcher	Emma Krikler
Illustrator	Richard Hull
Consultant	Matthew Oates
	Zoologist

© Aladdin Books 1990

First published in
the United States in 1991 by
Gloucester Press
387 Park Avenue South
New York, NY 10016

Library of Congress Cataloging-in-Publication Data

Hemsley, William.
    Jellyfish to insects : projects with science / William Hemsley.
      p. cm. -- (Hands on science)
    Includes index.
    Summary: Examines the anatomy, life cycles, and behavior of the
main groups of invertebrates. Includes experiments and projects
throughout.
    ISBN 0-531-17293-7
    1. Invertebrates--Juvenile literature. [1. Invertebrates. 2.
Invertebrates--Experiments. 3. Experiments.] I. Title. II. Series.
QL362.4.H46   1991
592'.0078--dc20   90-45657   CIP   AC

Printed in Belgium

HANDS · ON · SCIENCE

JELLYFISH TO INSECTS

William Hemsley

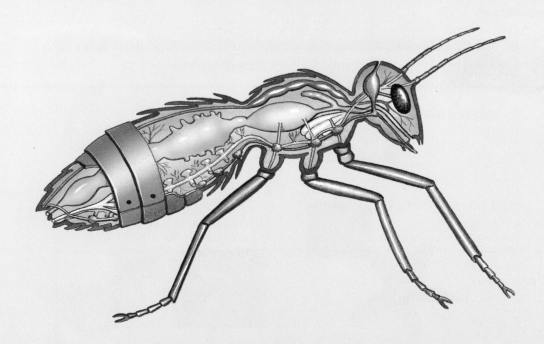

GLOUCESTER PRESS
London · New York · Toronto · Sydney

CONTENTS

This book is about a huge group of small animals that have no backbone. They are called invertebrates. They include worms, snails, shellfish, spiders and insects. Between them these creatures have conquered all the environments on Earth, from the tops of mountains to the depths of the seas. There are "hands on" projects for you to try and "did you know?" panels of information for fun.

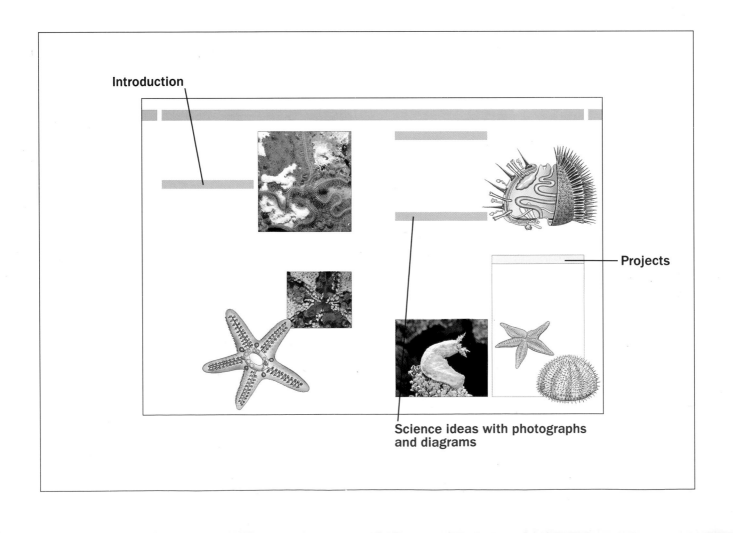

Introduction

Projects

Science ideas with photographs and diagrams

INTRODUCTION

The animal kingdom can be divided into two main groups: animals with backbones (vertebrates) and animals without backbones (invertebrates). This book is about invertebrates.

When we think of animals, we usually think of animals that are vertebrates. Vertebrates include mammals (such as dogs, lions and people), birds, reptiles, amphibians and fishes. But the great majority of animals in the world are invertebrates.

There are not only great numbers of invertebrates, but there are also very many different types. For example, there are more than one million known species of insects, and about 8,000 new species are discovered every year. There are about 4,000 species of mammals.

This book describes the most important groups of invertebrates. It tells you about some of their main features and ways of life, and what distinguishes one group from another.

This beetle shows all the typical features of an insect.

Jellyfish, sea anemones, corals and hydras all belong to a group of animals called the coelenterates. Coelenterates are very simple animals. They all live in water, and nearly always in seawater. They have a strange life cycle in which they live in two quite different forms: polyps and medusas.

JELLYFISH

Jellyfish, like other coelenterates, are made up of two layers of cells: the outer layer is for protection, and the inner layer is the lining of the stomach. Between these layers is a jellylike material, called mesoglea. This usually makes up most of the animal. Jellyfish vary in size from a few millimeters to three feet across.

Jellyfish are carnivores — that is, they eat animals. They have tentacles around their mouth. The tentacles catch prey and draw it into the mouth. They have special cells called nematocysts. Some nematocysts sting and paralyze prey; others are very sticky and catch hold of the jellyfish's prey.

△ Coral is formed by some species of polyp. The polyps build limestone skeletons. When they die, new polyps add more limestone.

▽ Medusas produce an egg that develops into a larva called a planula. This attaches to a rock and grows into a polyp. The polyp grows new medusas, which break off.

▽ This jellyfish is at the medusa stage of its life cycle. It spent the first part of its life as a polyp, which looked very different.

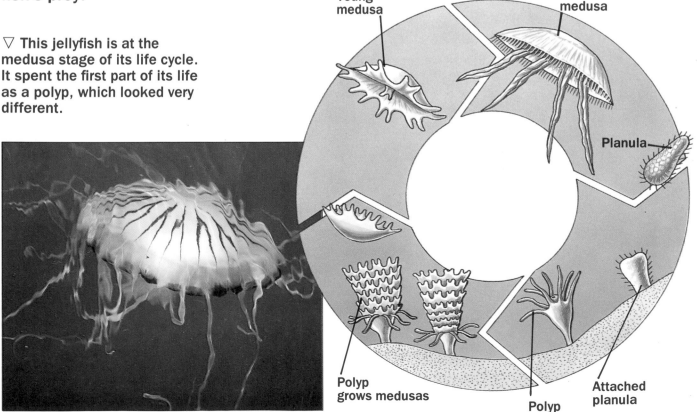

Young medusa

Adult medusa

Planula

Polyp grows medusas

Polyp

Attached planula

SEA ANEMONES

Sea anemones are brightly colored and look like flowers growing in the sea. They vary in size from a few millimeters to about three feet across. Anemones live attached to rocks, although they can move around slowly.

Sea anemones are a type of polyp. They do not have a medusa stage in their life cycle. They produce tiny new anemones, called budding, which break off from the parent. Sometimes sea anemones split down the middle, called fission, and the two halves separate.

Like jellyfish, sea anemones have tentacles covered in nematocysts. When prey comes too close, it is paralyzed. Sticky nematocysts hold the prey. The prey is then drawn down into the gut.

HYDRAS

Hydras are unusual coelenterates because they live in fresh water. Hydras are polyps. Like sea anemones, they do not have a medusa stage.

Hydras look rather like thin sea anemones with long tentacles. They are rarely more than ⅓ inch long. Hydras live attached to rocks and plants. They catch tiny plants and animals with their tentacles, which have nematocysts.

Hydras attach themselves by what is known as a basal disc at the bottom of their bodies. They can move slowly by walking on this disc. But if a hydra needs to move more quickly, it bends over and its tentacles take hold of a hard surface. The basal disc then lets go, and the hydra turns a cartwheel!

▽ The basic structure of sea anemones is like that of other coelenterates. Two layers of cells surround the gut.

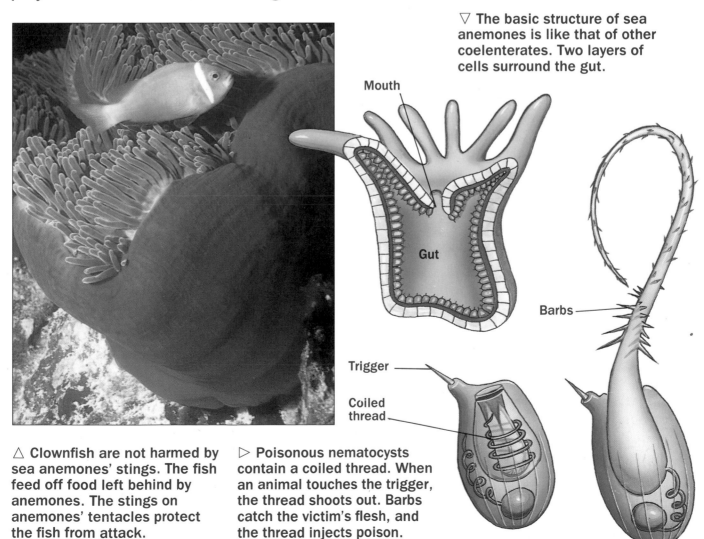

Mouth

Gut

Barbs

Trigger

Coiled thread

△ Clownfish are not harmed by sea anemones' stings. The fish feed off food left behind by anemones. The stings on anemones' tentacles protect the fish from attack.

▷ Poisonous nematocysts contain a coiled thread. When an animal touches the trigger, the thread shoots out. Barbs catch the victim's flesh, and the thread injects poison.

There are four main types of worm: flatworms, ribbon worms, roundworms and segmented worms. Worms have soft bodies which are usually long and thin. They have no legs. The main senses they use are touch and the ability to detect chemicals that are around them. Many have simple eyes or light-sensitive spots.

FLATWORMS

Flatworms are also known as platyhelminths. As the name flatworm suggests, most of them have flat bodies, which are often leaf-shaped. Their bodies have a simple structure with three layers. There is an outer layer that forms the skin of the animal. The inner layer forms the intestine. And there is a middle layer of muscles and other organs between the inner and outer layers.

Many types of flatworm are parasites. Parasites live on or in an animal or plant, which is known as the host. Parasites get their food by feeding off the host.

Other flatworms live in water. These are called turbellarians. They are usually found in the mud or living among the tiny plants at the bottom of the water.

FLUKES

Flukes are parasitic flatworms. They are leaf-shaped and have suckers and hooks to attach themselves to their host. Some flukes cause little damage, but others can kill their host.

Several types of flukes infect mammals. The adult flukes can live in the human intestine and bladder, where they mate. Eggs pass out of the body with feces. The eggs hatch into larvae called miracidia, which live in water. The larva burrow into snails, where they produce hundreds of another form of larva, called cercariae. The cercariae leave the snail and again live in water. They can then burrow through the skin of a host.

△ Most turbellarians, such as this one, live in water, but a few live on land. Turbellarians are the only group of flatworms that are not parasites.

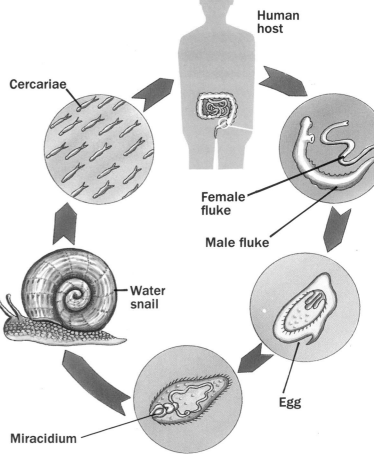

Human host

Cercariae

Female fluke

Male fluke

Water snail

Egg

Miracidium

△ The blood fluke causes the disease bilharzia (also called schistosomiasis) in humans, particularly in Africa.

TAPEWORMS

Tapeworms are another group of parasitic flatworms. The adult lives in the intestine of its host (for example, a human) and absorbs digested food. The body of a tapeworm has three parts: a head, a neck and a body. The head has hooks and suckers, which hold on to the intestine wall of the host. The body grows many segments. Each forms sacks of eggs. The end segments drop off and leave the host with feces. They then release the eggs. The eggs enter a second host (for example, a pig), usually in drinking water, and hatch into larvae. The larvae burrow from the host's intestine into its flesh. If a human eats the flesh (and it has not been properly cooked), a larva can form into a new adult.

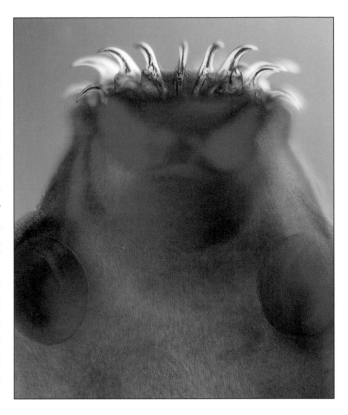

△ Tapeworms have no eyes on their heads, and their other senses are poor. When living in an intestine, they do not have to look for food or watch out for danger.

▽ The pork tapeworm has humans and pigs as hosts.

Larva

Human

Infected pork

Embryo grows into larva

Egg

Segment with eggs

Embryo

Pig

DID YOU KNOW?

Most flatworms are less than two inches long. Some tapeworms are this length, and have just four segments. But tapeworms can be over 100 feet long. They grow to almost the length of the intestine they are living in. New segments are added from the neck, so the oldest segments are farthest from the head.

Ribbon worms, roundworms and segmented worms are more complex in their structure than flatworms. They have better developed nerve and blood systems. Roundworms and segmented worms have a fluid-filled cavity around the intestine. This gives them four instead of three layers in their structure.

RIBBON WORMS

Ribbon worms are also called nemertines. They are usually quite small (two inches long or less), although the bootlace worm can grow to several feet in length. Most of them live in the sea, but a few live in fresh water or on land. They feed on small animals such as mollusks or other worms.

Ribbon worms have an unusual way of catching food. A tube shoots out through a special pore in the head. The tube is made to shoot out when the worm fills it with fluid. In some ribbon worms, the tube wraps around the prey. In others the tube has spikes and stabs the victim. A few have tubes that can sting.

ROUNDWORMS

Roundworms are also called nematodes. They have narrow, round bodies that get thinner at the ends. Some are very small, but the largest can be three feet long.

Many roundworms live in the soil or in water. These feed off the dead remains of plants and animals. Other roundworms live as parasites on plants and animals, and some can cause serious diseases.

Many species of roundworm infect people. The ascaris roundworm breeds in the human intestine and produces eggs. The eggs leave the intestine with feces. They can then get into the food of cattle and pigs. The eggs hatch into larvae in the animal's intestine. The larvae burrow out of the intestine and into muscle. This may then be eaten by a human host.

△ This ribbon worm is one of the few that live on land.

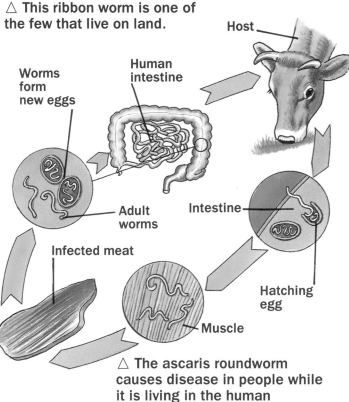

Host

Worms form new eggs

Human intestine

Adult worms

Intestine

Hatching egg

Infected meat

Muscle

△ The ascaris roundworm causes disease in people while it is living in the human intestine.

△ Tentacles on a polychaete.

◁ Leeches do not feed often. But when they do, they can drink more than their own body weight in blood.

SEGMENTED WORMS

Segmented worms are often called annelids. The segments make them look as if they are made of a series of rings.

One group of segmented worms lives in or near the sea. This group is called the polychaetes (pronounced *poli-keets*). They have long tentacles around their mouth. They use these to gather particles of food from the water.

A second group is called the oligochaetes. This group includes the earthworms. Earthworms move through the soil eating dead plant material. They are important to farmers and gardeners because they break up the soil. This lets water and air into the ground.

The third group is the leeches. These are parasites that suck blood from animals. Their bodies are quite flat, and they have suckers to hold on to their host. Most leeches live in water.

EXPERIMENT

You can watch earthworms move through the soil. Get an adult to help make a narrow tank with glass sides. The tank can be held together with strong tape. Only the large sides have to be made of glass. Make sure that air can get in. Fill the tank with loose, damp soil. Find two or three worms and put them in the tank. Then watch. Remember to put the worms back where you found them after a few days.

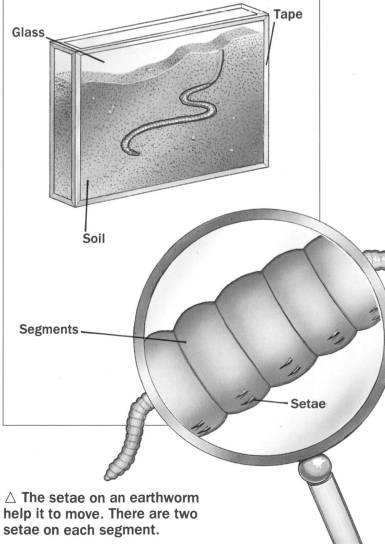

△ The setae on an earthworm help it to move. There are two setae on each segment.

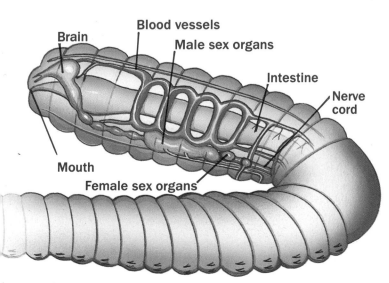

Starfish and sea urchins belong to a group called the echinoderms (pronounced *ekino-derms*), which means spiny-skinned. They are unusual because they are symmetrical in several different directions. They all live in the sea, sometimes in shallow water and sometimes in very deep oceans.

STARFISH

Starfish have five arms. But starfish move by walking on dozens of very small feet. These feet are tubes. Each tube foot moves when water is pumped in and out of it. A system of canals carries water to the feet. There are pumps on the canals. These control how the water moves. Starfish suck water in from the sea through a filter.

Starfish feed mainly on shellfish, such as mussels and scallops. A starfish first pulls the shell of its prey open just a crack. Then the starfish turns its stomach inside out through its mouth and pushes the stomach into the shell. The stomach then digests the victim.

If a starfish is caught by one arm, it escapes by letting the arm drop off. A new arm grows in its place.

△ Brittle stars are relatives of starfish. But their arms are much longer than those of starfish. They move by walking with their arms instead of by using tube feet.

▷ The system of water-filled canals in a starfish moves the arms as well as controlling the tube feet.

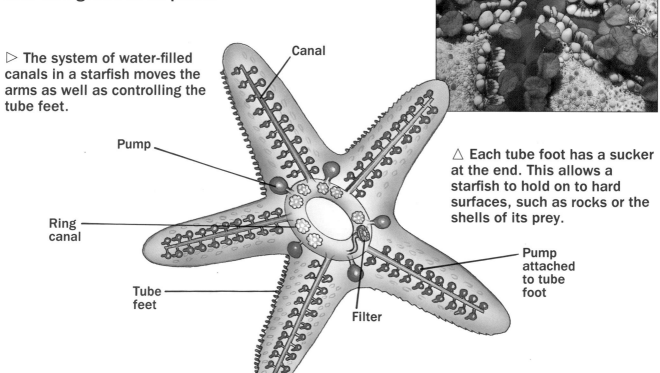

Canal

Pump

Ring canal

Tube feet

Filter

△ Each tube foot has a sucker at the end. This allows a starfish to hold on to hard surfaces, such as rocks or the shells of its prey.

Pump attached to tube foot

SEA URCHINS

Sea urchins live on rocky shores and in shallow water. They measure from one third to twenty inches across. Their bodies are surrounded by hard plates that make a shell. The shell is covered in spines. Sea urchins have a mouth with teeth. They feed on tiny plants and animals. Some also have pincers on stalks. These can catch particles of food and pass them down to the mouth. Like starfish, sea urchins have tube feet.

SEA CUCUMBERS

Sea cucumbers are echinoderms with soft bodies. They are symmetrical in the same way as the other echinoderms, but this is quite difficult to see. They usually live buried in sand, which they burrow into using their tube feet. Sea cucumbers use tube feet near the mouth for gathering food. Some species leave these feet sticking out of the sand to collect particles of food from the water. Other species eat dead material that has sunk to the bottom of the sea.

▽ The tentacles on this sea cucumber are long tube feet, which it uses to catch food.

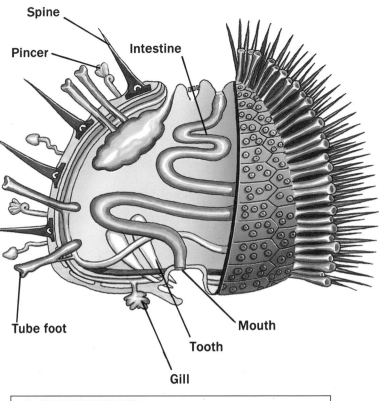

▽ Sea urchins breathe with small gills near to the mouth.

Spine

Pincer

Intestine

Tube foot

Mouth

Tooth

Gill

COLLECTING

You can collect the skeletons of starfish and sea urchins. The skeletons are the spiny skins or shells. They can be found on the seashore, especially in places where there are rocks (remember that rocks can be dangerous). The spines often fall off dead sea urchins, but be careful of living ones — the spines sometimes sting.

Starfish

Sea urchin

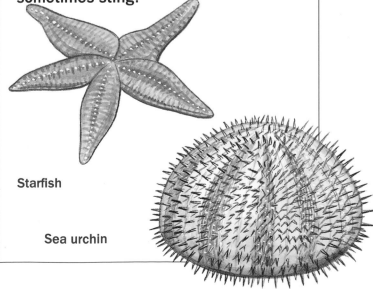

Mollusks are a large group of animals, with over 100,000 species. The word mollusk means soft-bodied, although many mollusks have a shell. There are three main groups of mollusks: gastropods, bivalves and cephalopods. The groups look quite different from each other, but have many things in common.

SNAILS

Gastropods are a group of mollusks that includes snails, slugs, limpets and periwinkles. Gastropod means stomach-foot. Many live on land, although some live in water. Gastropods either have one shell or no shell at all. Snails can pull their bodies inside their shells.

All gastropods have basically the same internal structure as a snail. Snails feed on plant material. Inside their mouths is a radula, which is like a tongue covered with teeth. They use this to scrape off particles of food. The food passes into the crop, where it is stored and digestion starts. The food then goes through a complex digestive system. Waste material from digestion passes out of the anus and the excretory pore. Snails breathe using a lung.

△ Limpets are a type of gastropod. They have powerful suckers underneath their bodies. They cling tightly to rocks on the seashore.

▽ Snails have two pairs of tentacles on their heads. These are snails' main sense organs. One pair has simple eyes, which can detect areas of light and dark.

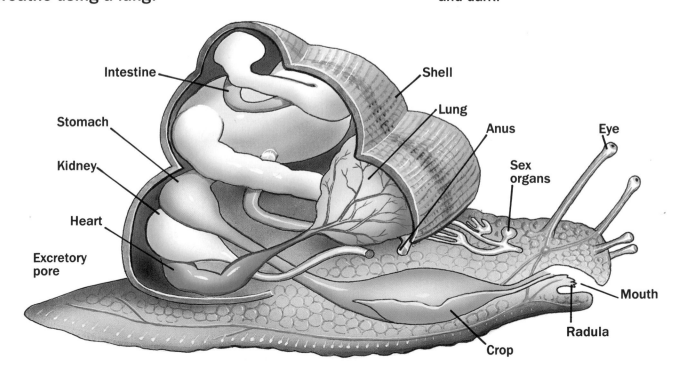

Intestine — Stomach — Kidney — Heart — Excretory pore — Crop — Radula — Mouth — Eye — Sex organs — Anus — Lung — Shell

MOVING

When slugs and snails move, muscles expand and contract along the bottom of the animal. This moves first one section along, then another. Gastropods secrete mucus to make movement easier. This mucus is slippery under parts of the foot that are moving. But it becomes solid under contracted parts so that the snail can grip to the ground. You can often see shiny trails of dried mucus that slugs or snails have left behind.

MATING

Snails and slugs are hermaphrodites. This means that all snails are both male and female at the same time. When two snails mate, the first thing they do is fire "love darts" into each other's bodies. These contain chemicals that stimulate mating. Sperm is then passed from each snail to the other. The eggs inside both bodies are fertilized. Once the eggs have been laid, they hatch into tiny snails.

△ Sea slugs are a group of gastropods that live in the salt water of seas and oceans. They have no shells and are often brightly colored.

▷ Some species of snail die after they have mated and then laid their eggs.

▽ Although slugs and snails move very slowly, some species of slug can climb as much as 30 feet up trees.

DID YOU KNOW?

When snails grow, one side of their bodies grows faster than the other. This is to make it fit into the spiral-shaped shell.

Because slugs have no shells and wet skins, there is always a risk of their drying out. This is why they always live in damp places.

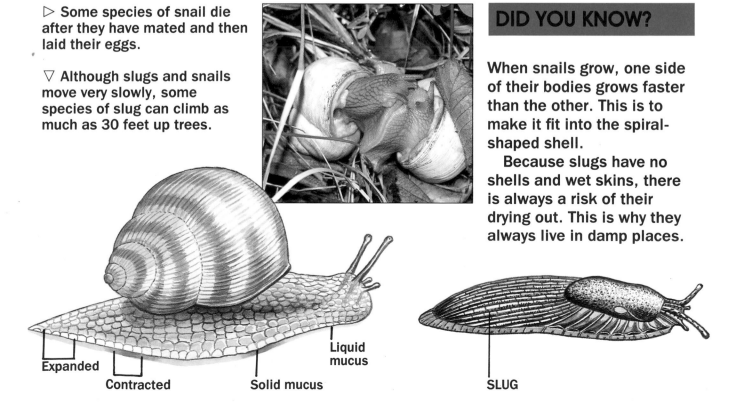

Expanded | Contracted | Solid mucus | Liquid mucus

SLUG

Bivalves are mollusks that have two separate shells (bivalve means two-shelled). These shells hinge together. Examples are mussels, cockles, clams and oysters. Most bivalves live in the sea, but a few live in fresh water. Like some other types of mollusk, many bivalves are eaten by people.

FILTER FEEDERS

Bivalves get their food by filter-feeding. They have special gills that are covered in tiny hairs called cilia. The cilia move in a way that draws water into the shell through a tube known as a siphon. Particles of food in the water are trapped by sticky mucus, which is produced by the gills. Movements of the cilia pass the particles down to the mouth. The water leaves through another siphon.

Some bivalves can move using a foot, and scallops can swim. But many never move. Oysters cement themselves onto rocks, and mussels attach themselves with strong threads. At one time, people made clothes from these threads.

△ Scallops swim by opening their shells then clapping them shut to send out a jet of water.

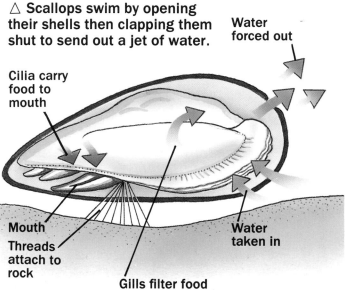

Cilia carry food to mouth

Water forced out

Mouth

Threads attach to rock

Water taken in

Gills filter food

▽ Clams burrow into sand for safety. The foot pushes down into the sand (A). Blood pumps into the end of the foot, which expands to make an anchor (B). Muscles shorten the foot to pull the clam down (C). The foot is pushed down to repeat the process (D). Water pumped through the siphons and the gap between the shells loosens the sand.

△ The mussel is a typical example of a bivalve. It feeds by filtering water, although it has less well-developed siphons than other bivalves.

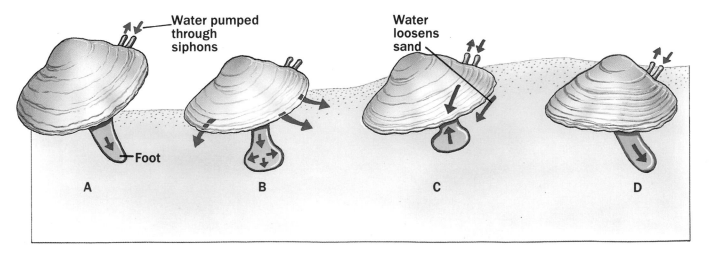

Water pumped through siphons

Foot

Water loosens sand

A   B   C   D

FOOD TEST

Discover what slugs and snails like eating. Find two or three gastropods. Put them into a box with a lid to stop them from escaping. An old shoe box is good. Put the box in the shade, somewhere that is not too hot, cold or dry. Now put various kinds of plant food into the box. (If you use food from the kitchen, make sure that it was going to be thrown away.) Cut the food so that it is all about the same size (get an adult to help with this). You will then be able to tell how much has been eaten.

What food do the animals like eating? Which food do they eat the most? Try the experiment first with one sort of gastropod, then with another.

Do not keep the animals for more than two or three days. Remember to put them back just where you found them.

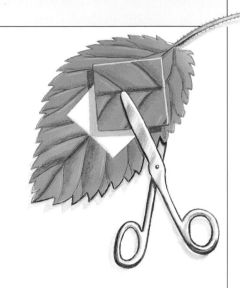

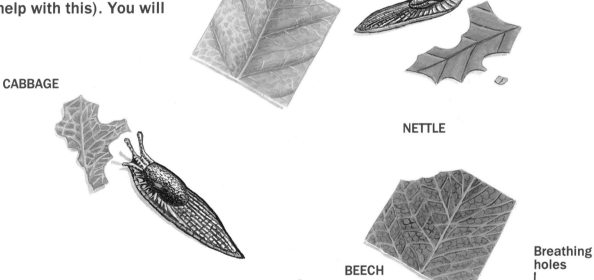

CABBAGE

OAK

NETTLE

BEECH

LETTUCE

MAPLE

Breathing holes

▷ Make sure that there are holes in the lid of your box so that the animals are able to breathe.

Cephalopods are the largest of the mollusks. Cephalopod means head-foot. There are three main groups: octopuses, squids and cuttlefish. None of these has any visible shell. They all have large heads with big eyes that give them good eyesight. They have several arms attached to the head.

JET-PROPELLED ANIMALS

Cephalopods move by jet propulsion. They squirt water out of the mantle cavity through the siphon. Squids and cuttlefish move mostly in this way, but octopuses usually walk using their arms.

Octopuses have eight arms. They use them to catch their prey, as well as for walking. The arms have suckers which can grip very strongly. Squids and cuttlefish have two long tentacles for catching prey as well as having arms.

Although cephalopods do not have visible shells, squids and cuttlefish do have a special sort of shell inside their bodies. These shells help to support the body and keep the animal afloat. In cuttlefish this is called the cuttlebone, and in squids it is called the pen.

When cephalopods are attacked, many of them release a jet of dark-colored ink to confuse the attacker. They can also change their color to camouflage themselves in different places.

△ Octopuses live in rocky areas near the shore where there are plenty of places to hide from danger and wait for prey.

▽ The cuttlefish has internal organs typical of cephalopods. The beak is used to attack prey. Octopus beaks can inject poison that is deadly to the small animals they attack.

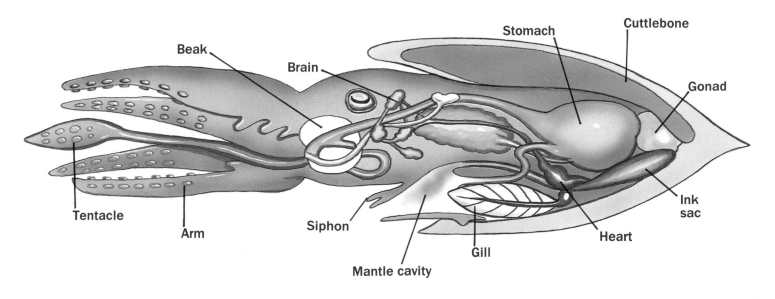

Beak

Brain

Stomach

Cuttlebone

Gonad

Tentacle

Arm

Siphon

Mantle cavity

Gill

Heart

Ink sac

COLLECTING AND IDENTIFYING SHELLS

If you go to the sea, you will find many shells of dead mollusks on the shore. You can also find mollusk shells on land or by fresh water. Can you tell what kind off mollusk the shell comes from? With bivalves — like clams — you will usually only find one of the two shells. See how many of the ones shown here you can find.

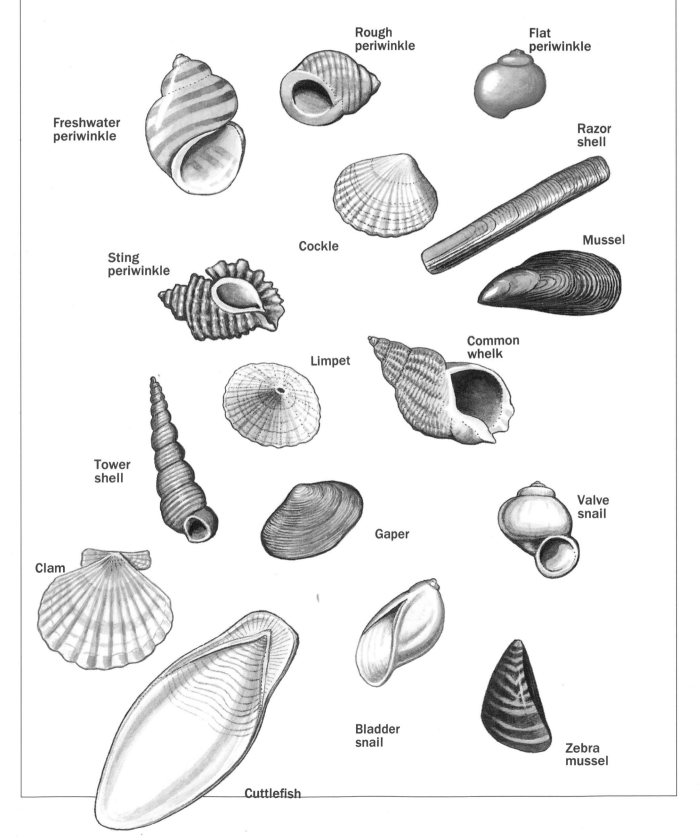

Rough periwinkle

Flat periwinkle

Freshwater periwinkle

Razor shell

Cockle

Mussel

Sting periwinkle

Common whelk

Limpet

Tower shell

Valve snail

Gaper

Clam

Bladder snail

Zebra mussel

Cuttlefish

Arthropods are the most common type of animal on earth. There are well over one million species, and four out of every five animals alive is an arthropod. They live in water and on land, and many can fly. Arthropod means joint-legged. Types of arthropod include crustaceans, arachnids and insects.

TEN LEGS

Crustaceans live in the sea. Large crustaceans, such as lobsters and crabs, usually have ten legs. But other species have more or fewer. One pair of legs often has claws attached. Crustaceans also have pleopods. These look slightly like legs, but have a different structure and different uses.

The whole body is covered with a hard skeleton. Muscles are attached to the inside of the skeleton. The body is usually divided into three main sections: the head, thorax and abdomen. The head has eyes called compound eyes. These are made up of many tiny eyes all clustered together. The head also has two pairs of antennae. The thorax contains most of the internal organs, such as the stomach and the sexual organs. The abdomen contains much of the intestine.

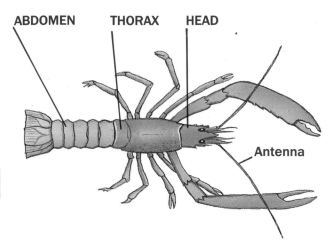

ABDOMEN   THORAX   HEAD

Antenna

5 legs each side

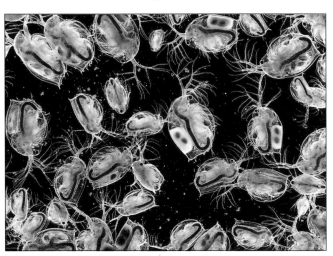

△ Water fleas are small crustaceans.

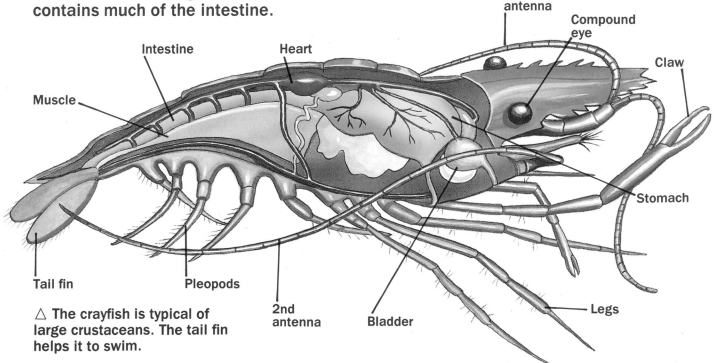

△ The crayfish is typical of large crustaceans. The tail fin helps it to swim.

Intestine   Heart

Muscle

Tail fin   Pleopods

2nd antenna   Bladder

1st antenna

Compound eye

Claw

Stomach

Legs

BARNACLES

Barnacles do not look like typical crustaceans. They live attached to hard surfaces, such as rocks or the hulls of ships. Barnacles attach themselves by a stalk called a peduncle. This is very short in some species and quite long in others. The peduncle has a cement gland that glues the barnacle down.

Barnacles have a shell-like plate called a carina. The plate opens to let out special netlike feet called cirri. These catch scraps of food floating in the water.

Barnacles mate by extending a long tube (penis) to neighboring barnacles. Sperm passes along the tube.

DID YOU KNOW?

Unlike most crustaceans, woodlice are unusual because they live on land. However, woodlice can dry out easily, so they do various things to keep moist. They live in damp places, such as dead wood, rotting leaves and under stones. They usually come out only at night to avoid the hot sun. They also roll themselves into balls. This saves water and is also a defense against enemies.

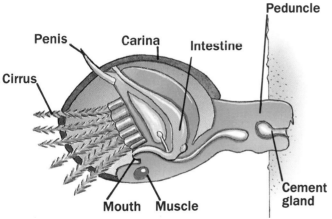

▽ Fiddler crabs are so called because their claws remind you of a violin and a bow.

The arachnids are a large group of arthropods that live on land. They include spiders, scorpions, and ticks and mites. Like all arthropods, arachnids have a hard external skeleton. The body is divided into two parts: a head and thorax that are joined together (the cephalothorax), and an abdomen.

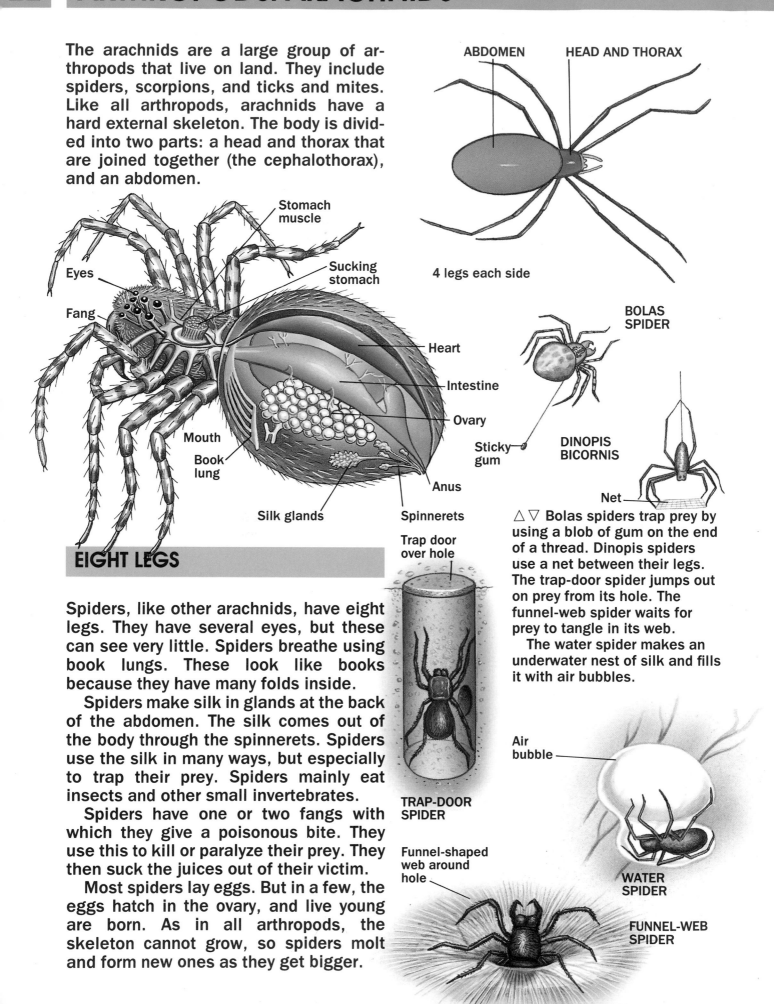

ABDOMEN   HEAD AND THORAX

4 legs each side

Stomach muscle

Eyes

Fang

Sucking stomach

Heart

Intestine

Ovary

Mouth

Book lung

Anus

Silk glands

Spinnerets

BOLAS SPIDER

DINOPIS BICORNIS

Sticky gum

Net

Trap door over hole

TRAP-DOOR SPIDER

Funnel-shaped web around hole

Air bubble

WATER SPIDER

FUNNEL-WEB SPIDER

EIGHT LEGS

Spiders, like other arachnids, have eight legs. They have several eyes, but these can see very little. Spiders breathe using book lungs. These look like books because they have many folds inside.

Spiders make silk in glands at the back of the abdomen. The silk comes out of the body through the spinnerets. Spiders use the silk in many ways, but especially to trap their prey. Spiders mainly eat insects and other small invertebrates.

Spiders have one or two fangs with which they give a poisonous bite. They use this to kill or paralyze their prey. They then suck the juices out of their victim.

Most spiders lay eggs. But in a few, the eggs hatch in the ovary, and live young are born. As in all arthropods, the skeleton cannot grow, so spiders molt and form new ones as they get bigger.

△▽ Bolas spiders trap prey by using a blob of gum on the end of a thread. Dinopis spiders use a net between their legs. The trap-door spider jumps out on prey from its hole. The funnel-web spider waits for prey to tangle in its web.

The water spider makes an underwater nest of silk and fills it with air bubbles.

SCORPIONS

Scorpions hunt by night for insects and spiders. They catch their prey with two powerful pincers, which they use to tear their victims apart. Scorpions have a sting in the end of their tails. If their prey puts up a fight, they curl the tail forward to sting it.

Most species of scorpion are not really dangerous to people. They will very rarely attack somebody deliberately. Many scorpions can give a nasty sting, however, and a few can be deadly.

Scorpions give birth to live young. The tiny scorpions then ride around on the mother's back. One mother can often carry as many as 30 of her babies.

△ There were scorpions very like this one living on Earth 450 million years ago.

TICKS AND MITES

Ticks and mites are very similar, but mites are larger. They look as if they only have one body segment. Most of them are parasites.

Ticks and mites have a mouth that has a beak with teeth. They use this to grab on to host animals, such as cats, dogs, fish, insects or people. They then suck blood or other fluids from the victim. Some species also feed off plants.

Ticks and mites can carry diseases, such as Rocky Mountain spotted fever. Some can get into the skin of humans and cause an irritating rash.

△ Mites are less than 0.04 in long.

DID YOU KNOW?

A spider starts its web by letting the wind blow a thread from one support to another (1). It then spins a second thread between the supports by crawling along the first thread (2). It pulls the second thread into a V-shape, which makes a basic frame (3). It then adds arms to complete the frame (4). The web is finished by joining all the arms together with a spiral (5). Building a web usually takes a spider about an hour.

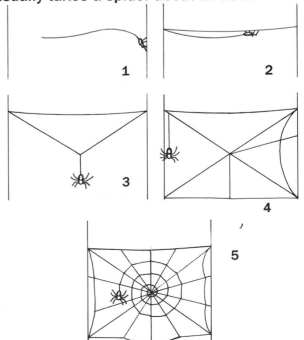

Insects are the largest group of arthropods. It is unusual to go through a day without seeing many insects. Flies, bees, ants, beetles, moths, butterflies and many other animals are all insects. They mostly live on land, and many can fly. Like other arthropods, they have a hard external skeleton.

SIX LEGS

Insects have three main body parts: the head, the thorax and the abdomen. They have six legs attached to the thorax, and usually have one or two pairs of wings.

The head has a pair of antennae. These act as sense organs to detect smell or movement. Insects have compound eyes, like those of crustaceans. Often they have simple eyes as well. Many insects have several other sense organs, such as special ears on their legs.

Insects breathe through holes in the sides of their bodies called spiracles. These are connected to tubes inside the body known as trachea. The trachea branch into many fine tubes. These take air to the organs of the body. Muscle movements in the abdomen make air move in and out of the spiracles.

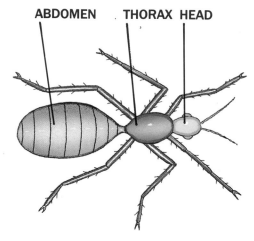

ABDOMEN   THORAX HEAD

3 legs each side

▽ This hover fly has a typical insect body structure.

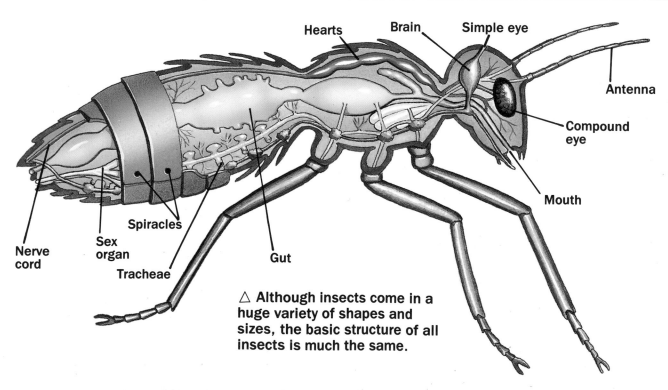

Hearts   Brain   Simple eye

Antenna

Compound eye

Mouth

Nerve cord

Sex organ

Spiracles

Tracheae

Gut

△ Although insects come in a huge variety of shapes and sizes, the basic structure of all insects is much the same.

GROWTH AND DEVELOPMENT

All insects start life as eggs. An egg laid by an adult hatches, and a new insect starts to develop. There are three ways in which insects develop into adults.

Some insects hatch as tiny versions of the adult. The external skeleton of the insect cannot grow. When the insect reaches a certain size, it molts, shedding its skeleton. A new, larger skeleton grows in its place. Each stage of growth is known as an instar.

Some insects go through what is known as incomplete metamorphosis. The egg hatches into a nymph. Some nymphs look very much like the adult, but without certain features, such as wings. Other nymphs look quite different, but change into an adult in the final stage of molting. The adult is called the imago.

Other insects go through complete metamorphosis. They hatch as larvae that look nothing like the adult. Some larvae look like worms; others have small legs. Once the larvae have grown, they transform into pupae. Pupae have protective coverings. Inside its covering an insect changes into an adult. When the change is complete, the covering opens and an adult emerges.

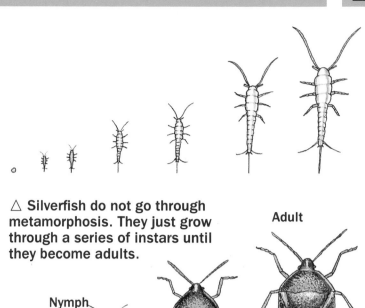

△ Silverfish do not go through metamorphosis. They just grow through a series of instars until they become adults.

Adult

Nymph

△ Beetles go through incomplete metamorphosis. Beetle's wings only appear in the adult stage.

Adult

Egg   Larva

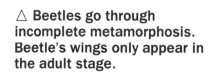
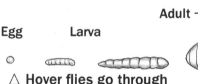

Pupa

△ Hover flies go through complete metamorphosis. The larva and pupa are completely different from the adult form of the insect.

△ Emerging from an old skeleton.

△ Emerging from a pupa case.

METAMORPHOSIS

You can watch metamorphosis in a butterfly for yourself. Find a caterpillar (a butterfly larva) and put it in a large glass jar. Put some food in the jar. The food must be the same kind of leaf as you found the caterpillar on. Many caterpillars will only eat one kind of leaf. Caterpillars eat a lot, so you may have to give it many leaves. Put a twig upright in the jar. When the butterfly appears, wait for the wings to expand and harden. Then return it to the place you found the caterpillar.

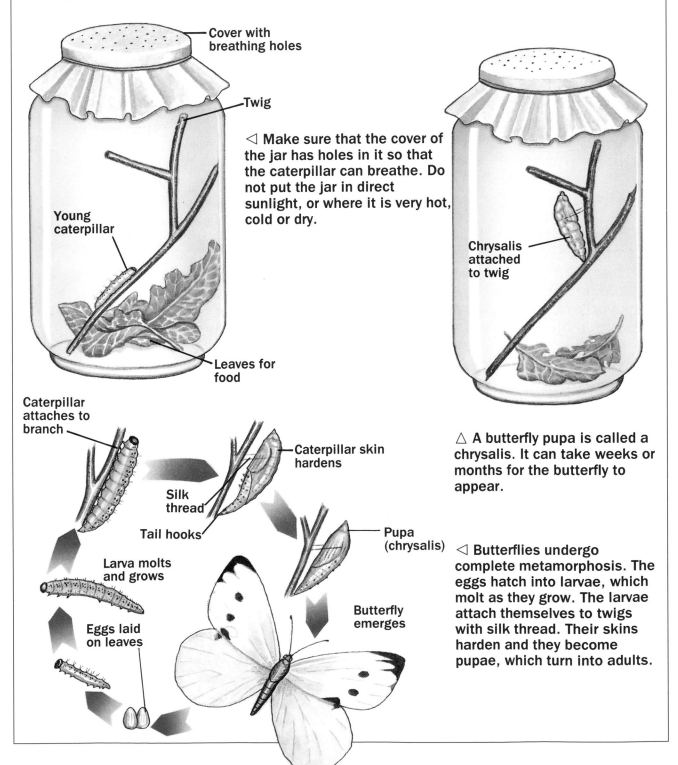

Cover with breathing holes

Twig

◁ Make sure that the cover of the jar has holes in it so that the caterpillar can breathe. Do not put the jar in direct sunlight, or where it is very hot, cold or dry.

Young caterpillar

Leaves for food

Chrysalis attached to twig

△ A butterfly pupa is called a chrysalis. It can take weeks or months for the butterfly to appear.

Caterpillar attaches to branch

Caterpillar skin hardens

Silk thread

Tail hooks

Larva molts and grows

Pupa (chrysalis)

Eggs laid on leaves

Butterfly emerges

◁ Butterflies undergo complete metamorphosis. The eggs hatch into larvae, which molt as they grow. The larvae attach themselves to twigs with silk thread. Their skins harden and they become pupae, which turn into adults.

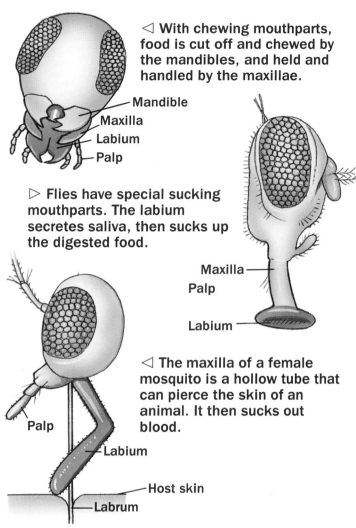

◁ With chewing mouthparts, food is cut off and chewed by the mandibles, and held and handled by the maxillae.

— Mandible
— Maxilla
— Labium
— Palp

▷ Flies have special sucking mouthparts. The labium secretes saliva, then sucks up the digested food.

Maxilla —
Palp

Labium —

◁ The maxilla of a female mosquito is a hollow tube that can pierce the skin of an animal. It then sucks out blood.

Palp
— Labium
— Host skin
— Labrum

FEEDING

Insects feed on a great variety of food and in very many ways. Each species has mouthparts that are specially designed for the way in which it feeds. There are two main types: chewing mouthparts and sucking mouthparts.

Insects with chewing mouthparts have two pairs of jaws: the mandibles and the maxillae. There are two lips: the labrum above the mouth and the labium below. The palps are used to taste food. Sucking mouthparts are a variation of chewing mouthparts, but are very much changed.

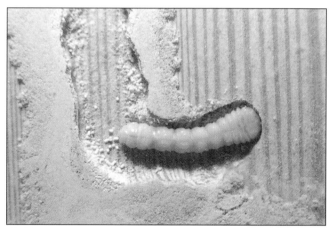

△ This lava can eat through wood.

FLYING

Many species of insect have wings. Flies have one pair of wings. They have special knoblike structures called halteres instead of rear wings. Halteres help them to balance. Beetles also have one pair of proper wings. Instead of front wings they have wing covers. Most other insects have two pairs of wings. These usually flap up and down together. Sometimes the wings on each side are joined together by special hooks along the edges.

The speed at which the wings of different insects flap varies. Some butterflies flap fewer than five times a second. Small flies flap up to 1,000 times per second. The fastest insect fliers are dragonflies, some of which can fly at 65 miles per hour.

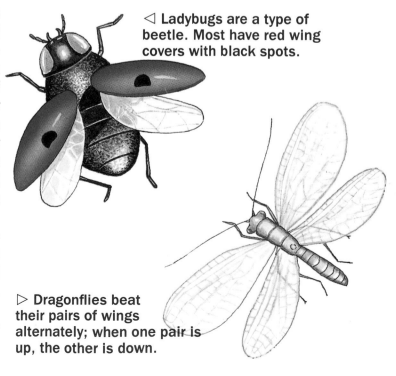

◁ Ladybugs are a type of beetle. Most have red wing covers with black spots.

▷ Dragonflies beat their pairs of wings alternately; when one pair is up, the other is down.

SOCIAL BEHAVIOR

Ants, termites, bees and some species of wasp live in large groups called colonies. Often these colonies build nests to live in. For example, African termites build nests that can be up to three times the height of a person.

The insects that live in a colony are divided into different types. Each type has a particular job. For example, some ant colonies have special "soldier ants," which have fierce jaws and protect the colony. In ant and bee colonies, it is the females who do all the work. The male's only job is to mate with the queen.

The queen is the female that lays all the eggs for the whole colony. The queen is often many times bigger than any other insect in the colony.

△ Soldier termites guard workers.

COMMUNICATION

Insects in colonies have to communicate with each other. This is so that the colony can run efficiently. For example, if one insect finds a supply of food, it needs to tell others so that they can help to carry it to the nest.

Insects in colonies communicate in several ways. Some do it by touch, for example, by putting their antennae together. Sound and smell are also used. The activities of a termite colony are controlled by special chemicals that are released by the queen. Bees have a dance that one bee performs to show the direction and distance of a supply of food it has found.

△ A colony of bees in its hive.

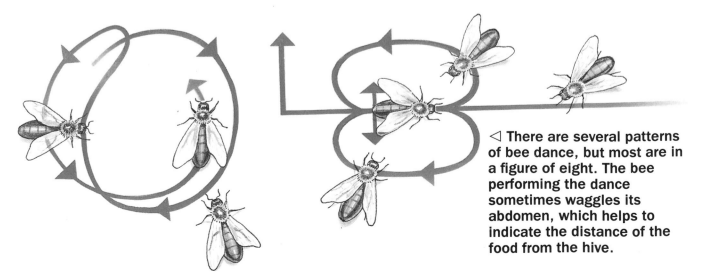

◁ There are several patterns of bee dance, but most are in a figure of eight. The bee performing the dance sometimes waggles its abdomen, which helps to indicate the distance of the food from the hive.

ANTS

When ants find a supply of food, they take as much of it as they can back to the ant nest.

If you see an ant, try to find out where its nest is. The entrance may be very small — for example, a crack between the pavement. Remember to be careful, because some types of ant can give a nasty bite.

Once you have found a nest, put some food down a few feet away from it. When one ant has found the food, it will tell others. A trail of ants will form, with some ants carrying food to the nest, and others walking back for more.

Once the ant trail has formed, try putting an obstacle like a twig across the trail. See how long it takes the ants to figure out how to cross it.

Are there any ants guarding the nest? Are any ants searching for more food?

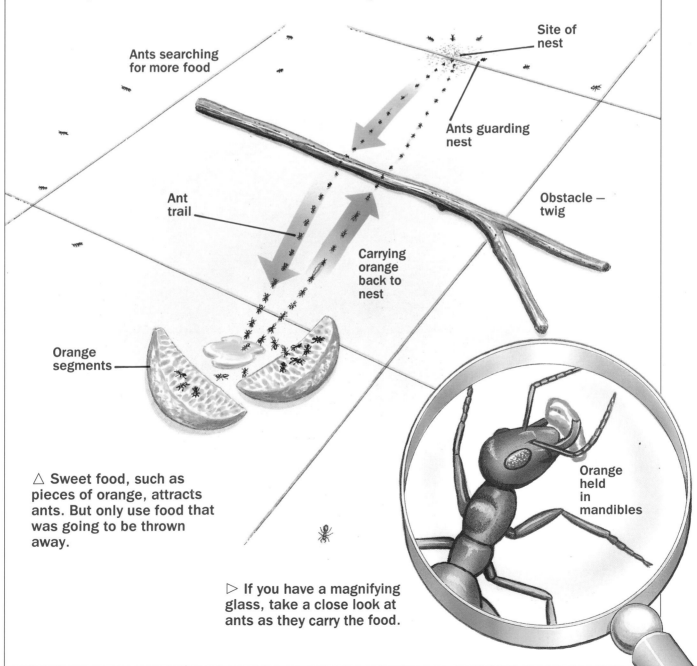

Ants searching for more food

Site of nest

Ants guarding nest

Ant trail

Obstacle — twig

Carrying orange back to nest

Orange segments

Orange held in mandibles

△ Sweet food, such as pieces of orange, attracts ants. But only use food that was going to be thrown away.

▷ If you have a magnifying glass, take a close look at ants as they carry the food.

This book has talked about the main groups of invertebrates. Each group is made up of species of animals that have many important features in common. Some groups are divided into smaller groups — for example, there are three main groups of mollusks. Putting species into groups in this way is called classification. The chart below shows how invertebrates are classified. At the top of the chart are the most complex invertebrates. At the bottom of the chart are the simplest. Protozoans are considered the simplest of all animals. Each consists of just one cell, or (like sponges) colonies of single-celled animals.

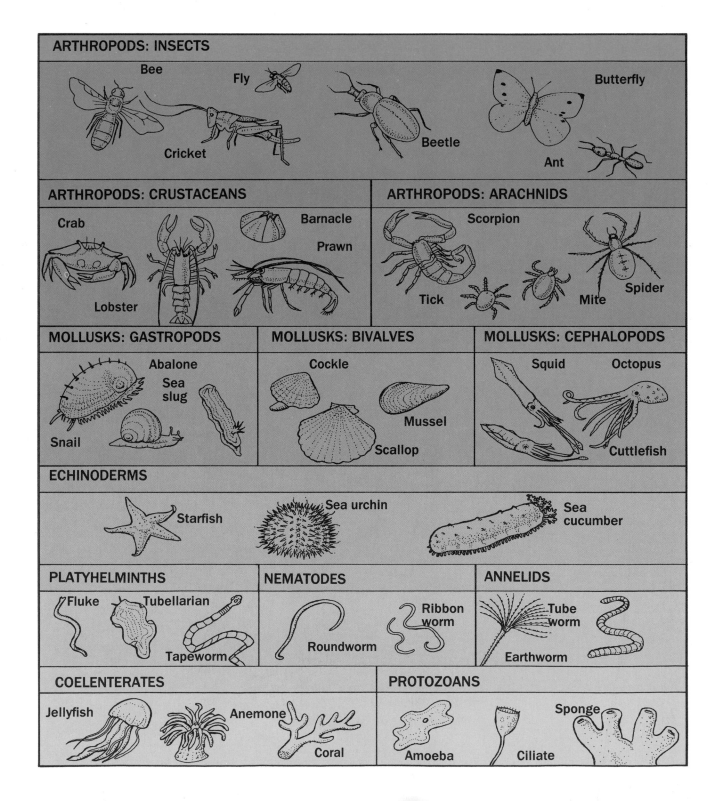

Antenna
A long thin organ that is attached to the head of an animal. Antennae are sense organs, which most usually detect touch or smell.

Backbone
Row of bones that runs along the back of an animal. The bones surround a bundle of nerves. Animals that have backbones are called vertebrates.

Cell
The tiny basic unit from which living things are made. Each cell is surrounded by a thin membrane that separates it from other cells. All animals (except protozoans) are made up of many cells.

Egg
Special cell that is produced by a female animal and is usually covered by a protective case. Fertilized eggs grow into young animals.

External skeleton
A hard covering on the bodies of arthropods. It holds the body in shape and protects it.

Feces
Waste material that passes out of an intestine.

Gill
A structure in an animal that absorbs oxygen from water. Most animals that live in water use gills to breathe.

Host
The animal or plant that a parasite lives inside.

Intestine
A tube inside animals in which food is digested (broken down and absorbed into the animal).

Lung
A structure in animals that absorbs oxygen from air. Some invertebrates that live on land use lungs to breathe.

Metamorphosis
The change from the young form of an animal to the adult form in animals where the young form is very different from the adult.

Mucus
A sticky or slippery substance produced by an animal.

Organ
A part of an animal that has a particular function, for example, a heart is an organ that pumps blood.

Ovary
The place in a female animal where eggs are produced.

Parasite
An animal that feeds off a living plant or animal. Parasites usually live inside the plant or animal they feed off.

Penis
The part of a male animal that passes sperm to a female.

Sense organ
A part of an animal that is used to detect things in the animal's surroundings, for example, eyes or ears.

Sperm
Special cell produced by a male animal. It joins with an egg before the egg starts to grow into a new animal.

Tissue
A group of many cells that make up an organ in an animal, for example, heart tissue.

Photographic Credits:
Cover and pages 5, 6 top, 7, 9, 10 bottom, 12 top and bottom, 14, 15 top and bottom, 21 bottom, 23 top and bottom, 24 and 25 left and right: Planet Earth Photographic Library; pages 6 bottom, 8, 10 top, 11, 13, 16, 18, 20, 21 top, 27 and 28 top and bottom: Bruce Coleman Photo Library.